Misfit Tales

By Nikki Avila

Published by Paradisiac Publishing in Davenport, Iowa.
www.paradisiacpublishing.com

For more information, please contact:
paradisiacpublishing@gmail.com

Printed in the United States of America.

BISAC Category: Poetry/General

Avila, Nikki (author)
Misfit Tales
ISBN: **978-0692973806**

To Jon,

Thank you for showing me

that inside every person is

a happy poem waiting to

be written.

A Note from the Author:

Dear Reader,

At first the order of poems might confuse you. It might come across as lazy, thoughtless and meaningless. I assure you it's not. There were many hours spent hunched of these poems, attempting to find just the right order. Order is important after all. It gives meaning to what otherwise would be a jumbled mess. But because my order is indeed odd, I'm here to explain it to you.

First, the hundreds, two-hundreds, and three-hundreds. They seem out of place. They are. Those poems were meant for another book at a different time. But we all know how that goes. Books get dismantled. Poems get shuffled. And messages come to light. I thought it would be interesting to place these very first of my poetic ramblings next to some more "refined" pieces. Interesting because they fit so nicely. This old version of myself still made sense with the new. That was altogether refreshing and worrisome. Had I changed at all? Was I capable of it? Alas, questions for another time and another book.

Each of the four-hundreds and five-hundreds were placed with great delicacy. I couldn't have you getting to melancholy or find yourself with no place to place a book mark (if you must). So short poems followed long, happy poems followed series of sad poems. Change is important. Life is a rollercoaster. And now this book is too.

And the end. Oh, the end. I kept these poems together for a few reasons. They were written in such rapid succession it seemed inappropriate to then tear them apart. They belonged together. They told a story together. They were my state of mind over a series of weeks. Rather regular weeks, I won't lie, but regardless these weeks brought forth such creativity that I was able to finish *Misfit Tales*.

Now I'm presenting it to you. I do hope you'll enjoy it.

With Love,

A Fellow Outcast

WARNING!

Not everything written
in this book is meant
to be understood. More
often than not it's meant
to be felt.

#268

I fear that this

secret notebook of mine

will always be

a secret

#440

Writing was my in the box and
out of the box. My comfortable
and uncomfortable. Odd to think
it can be both, but it most certainly
can. Sure, it's a balm to my wounds.
Soothing the aches and pains. But
first it opens them. Lets them shrivel
up in the air. Pens expose all I've
hidden from myself. All I wish
would stay hidden.

#445

There were no delusions of grandeur.

No need to claw my way to the top.

No desire to be in charge of anyone but me.

It wasn't about glorified green paper.

Or people I've never met liking stuff people I know love.

It had only and would only be about the words. And their ability to unravel me like string.

Stitch me together and shape me into new and better things.

#453

It was easier for her, less awkward and a hell of a lot more comfortable to express herself through type. In person she found it difficult to form her churning emotions into sensible words. They became dirt in her mouth. Reeking of decay. A shadow of the once beautiful petals that were thought. Jumbled they tumbled out of her mouth, senseless. Letters afforded her a sense of control. A moment to compose the turmoil into something the living could digest.

#458

She had an addiction to beginnings and
a severe dislike of endings. It's why she
lingered over finished books. Analyzing
every word and scene. Contemplating
rereading every page. What she knew
had to be better than the mystery the
next novel presented.

#466

There's too much to me.
Empty spaces that need
Something, something.
I can't quite grasp it yet.
People or places, maybe
things. Possibly me.
Rooms that need occupants.
I'm a house, not a home.
Not quite yet.

#496

Here's the truth:
We're all a little
insecure. It's how
we deal with it
that defines our
confidence.

#497

I think I get it now.

The need to self-mutilate.

There's a release in it.

In that kind of control.

Being victim and perpetrator.

I know it now.

It's what I've been doing all along,

Bleeding myself dry for the words.

#500

Living's a little too much I think.

A tad bit more than I can handle.

Death's embrace was cold but constant.

This Life shit. An undulating frenzy.

A drug with too many repercussions.

Just not my style.

Existing sings a sweeter song.

#285

There's a downfall to loving
with your whole existence…

when that flame dies, so do you

#513

I'm crazy, right?

Certifiably insane.

Straight jackets and IV's.

To suppress the fantasies they say.

But that's not right. Can't be.

Insane is doing the same thing again and again.

Like this schedule they put me on.

Eat, sleep, repeat.

Medication for the dreams.

Don't dream.

It's different and different is insane.

So they say. They're not right.

Can't be.

Insane is expecting different from the same.

Eat, sleep, repeat. Repeat.

Re –

Bloods everywhere, the IV's gone

and the dreams are back.

If this is insane, truly manic,

then I think I like it.

#518

Rotting flesh.

A decomposing smile.

The decaying aroma of happiness.

I did it. I fit.

Right into this coffin.

#282

I wasn't anti-social.

Just anti-hate.

Turns out that leaves

you alone more often

than not.

#523

Maybe I couldn't let go of the past any more than I could stop breathing. Perhaps each memory was in my makeup now. Right down to the way I held myself: hunched over waiting for the blow that would always come.

And maybe you never really grow out of your old self. Maybe if you were the target once, you always would be.

#524

I suppose I could save us
all a lot of trouble if I came
with a warning sign:

I am not mindless reading.
Do not pick me up to pass
the time.

#532

It's okay that you're happy. That you're so content
you want to scream. Comfortable is uncomfortable
for you. I understand. It's strange, it's different.
You're not used to it. So scream. Scream until your
throat is raw and then continue to be content, darling.
Because this is okay. I promise.

#536

I think my mind

hurts me more

than other people do.

Causing the pain

before they can.

#539

Do not paint me the colors

you think I should be.

I am a master piece

as I am.

#560

Like a flower grown in the cracks of

the asphalt she was of the resilient kind.

Bendable, breakable, but absolutely beautiful.

No matter the brutality of winter she

always found a reason to greet the sun.

#563

Some people don't deserve a bridge.

They either haven't earned or already destroyed

their place in your life.

So don't give them another way in.

Not a backdoor. Not a window. Shut it all.

Any other available option.

And then burn it down.

All the connections they made.

All the bridges that span from their life to yours.

Watch them crumble.

Then walk away.

#588

I was dead.

To you.

And it was excruciating.

At least a real demise

allows victims to

fade into that dark void.

But I was painfully

aware of the blood

in my veins.

It marked me alive

when I'd rather

anything but.

That was an alone

I could handle.

#438

You said you'd surely die
without me. A prophecy to
be filled by your own hands.

But what of me? And all the
pieces lost with every second
my oxygen mixes with yours.

Don't you know a dead hostage
is a useless one?

#441

Beneath the self-loathing
and supposed memory loss,
under the grief and far below
the words, deeper than even
the poems, was a little girl
whose only wish was that
you could've loved her back.

How much easier it would've
been.

How less terribly lonely.

#442

It was one of those pictures you just had to see. Those that found their way into history books. Up there with MLK giving a speech and Einstein sticking out his tongue. The image alone could inspire awe and devotion. The person? Had a way of upturning lives. Helen of Troy, her face could start wars. Or end them if she only smiled as she was now.

#447

They had vicious views, deluded daydreams,
petulant prides. A preconceived notion that
birds were indeed fragile. With their hollow
bones and delicate digestion. Small, tiny,
unimportant things.

Twice as broad. More capable than others
artfully crafted arms. Layered of small, tiny,
unimportant things – feathers. With their
hollow bones and lighter than air feel, they
allowed her to fly.

There was no "actually" about it.
Though little, she was wild, and wild has
a way of doing what it does best: soaring.

#542

People don't choose me.
They choose the idea
of me that they want.

And now I don't know
who I am anymore.

#572 "Yes, You"

You're not bad or wrong or difficult. You're just
inconceivably different. You're beyond the stars and
planets. You transcend the Milky Way. You're the
beauty we can't look at. Partially because we're unable,
but mostly because we are too afraid. You hold in you
answers to every question we could ever have. You are
creation and death. Yet, our own insecurities keep us
from knowing what you'll bring. But don't be sad.
Someday, someone will look upon you. They'll see the
craters and cracks, the peaks and valleys. They'll dive in
your ocean and backstroke across your lakes. They'll
colonize the planet you are but leave you wild.
Someday, someone will love all there is to love. They
will kiss away your insecurities and make love to your
fear. They will take the danger out of loving with a
fierceness that exhaust, because they will too.

#439 "In Time"

I might not love me,

not yet.

But I like me.

For now that is enough.

#443

Hope was my only enemy

and how close I kept it.

#449

I've begun to realize I love Love.
The mere idea that someone out there –
unsatisfied atoms screaming –
is blindly following their disenchanted
heart strings to me, tantalizes.
That I might too silence the
incessant push and pull of my existence
provokes.

What a treat it would be to find home.

#287

Sure, opposites attract, but there's something appealing about magnets facing the same way. The push and pull. How t a n t a l i z i n g...

#467

Oddly enough, more often than not,
alone was all that made sense. In the
way empty made you full. Filling spaces
that didn't exist for other such nonsense
like happiness.

#477

What was human if not weak?

Living a life aimed only at finding

insubstantial emotions in

fleeting moments of understanding.

Craving affection demonstrated

through needless touching

and meaningless words.

What was life if not human?

An emotionless, colorless void.

A life without moments.

An absence of sense.

A meaningless string of now's.

#495

He wanted the truth

but didn't want to hear it.

"Don't go"

is all she wished

to say.

#501

I am no type.

None at all.

I am the blank canvas

you wish to fill with

your vibrant colors.

I am a blank page

eager for your words.

I am no type.

But I might be yours.

#166

A singular glance from you
set my blood on fire. It raged,
looking for an outlet
lest it burn me, but with none
it devoured me, from the inside
out.

And now I'm no more than a
pile of ashes drifting in the wind.

#503

You didn't want to be alone

and I wanted to be with you.

Somehow the space between

spoke all the difference of the two.

#511

You did it, didn't you? Just like that
you slipped inside. No pain. You're not
the first. But the pleasure? Oh, you were
different. It wasn't the immediate
fleeting feeling I was used to. It lingered.
And so did you.

#178

I knew better.

So did my head

and, surprisingly,

so did my heart.

But my feet,

my stupid feet,

tripped over themselves

anyway.

#515 "It Takes Two"

Have you ever tried to resist the beat? To ignore the furious flurry of your heart as the notes coil around you and yours. Attempting to be partners without touching. Sway before palms meet. Pirouette before the kiss.

Have you ever tried to dance around it? Feelings bright enough the sun would hide its face. It's agonizing.

#577 "Reflection"

We are, each and every one of us, a way station for lost souls.

We collect strays and pretend they are pets. That we each are domesticated enough to stay.

But we are all too busy searching to stay. Searching for that some place, some person, something that will feel like home.

If we are lucky enough, each and every one of us, will realize home was staring back at is in the mirror every day.

#596 "The Me I Am"

I don't want to be my insecurities.

My failures. My fears.

I don't want to be the thoughts

I have when I go quiet in a room full of noise.

I want to be my confidence.

My successes. My dreams.

I want to be my laughter

In a quiet room.

I want to be the me

I am with you.

#175

My dreams paled in comparison

to the reality you created

#444

I loved you enough for the both of us. Feverishly
making my heart beat for two. Exhausting my lungs,
pumping in air not only for me but for you too. And
what did that give me? A love enough for the both of
us but given all to you.

#448

It's frightening how I can shut it all off.

Flip the switch.

Dim the light.

Steal humanity with a thought.

It's so devastatingly easy.

The annihilation of feeling.

#464

She didn't have the advantage others did. Shutting
the door to chaos was beyond her. Not because it
followed her, but because it was her. One in the same,
neither could exist without the other.

#478

I met you

and tomorrow

became something

to look forward to

#475

Missing people was beyond her.

A feeling she couldn't grasp.

You didn't miss beating hearts

when your own was home.

#489 "273.5"

You toed the line.

Straddled it occasionally.

But never crossing. Not quite.

Nothing tangible anyway.

Without evidence, I questioned the validity of my claims, of my emotions.

Surely, if I couldn't see them no one else would believe me.

#173

my eyes couldn't hide

what my lips attempted to

your betrayal was more than

a false smile could fix

#504

I cannot argue any longer.
Not because I have no opinions
I have no wish to share.

I cannot argue because I think
you must be angry to do so and
my fire burned out ages ago.

I'm much too exhausted
to continue on with
petty squabbling.

#502

How heartbreaking

to have a skill

not in demand

Oh, how I could've

loved you

#499

Happiness is fleeting.

Give me pain.

That will always

be my home…

#528

There was a time when I wanted nothing more than to belong. To fit. To have a place I could call home. Now I wish only for oblivion. To have a mind free of the past. To forget those things you just can't not remember. The way it feels, an emotional punch to the gut, when you know you've been lied to. I want to erase your face and your words and your every touch. I need a clean slate. I need to start over. You're gone and I'm still suffocating in the memories. Screw belonging. Give me freedom.

#559

In everything you took there was
something you gave. It was a small
something. Hardly noticeable.
Just a minute character flaw
your actions imbedded in my being.
Compassion.

It was okay. I didn't blame you.

#561

Sometimes it does work out. Occasionally,
the stars align for that one perfect opportunity
that changes your world. But you'd never know
that if you didn't take the chance.

You were my chance.

#566

I'm the dark of the tunnel.

The weight on your shoulders.

I'm the discomfort in your belly

and the catch in your throat.

I'm the riptide and

the stagnant water.

Terrifying change and

gross stability.

I'm choice.

Make one.

#209

can you taste my pain

when I kiss you? are my lips

a testament to fear? Fear

that this is the last they'll

know yours…

#578 "This, This. That, That."

I hope one day I'll stop being so damn scared. I hope all the unnecessary worries will die. That I'll cease to wonder if this kiss will be our last. Or this one. Or that one. I want to quit holding you as if it's goodbye when all we said was hello.

#581 "Beautiful Messes"

I think that you were whole and when we met I was
only leftovers of people I knew and pieces of who I
had been. I think that you thought you'd be saving
me and I thought you'd be fixing me. Turns out we
were both wrong.

You were the one who needed saving all along. You
needed to be taught that beautiful messes were just
that: beautiful. And if given the chance, you could be
a mess too.

#182 "Mine"

I'd choose hell a thousand times over.

Suffer through all nine circles. Again and again.

Be tortured. Flayed. Quartered.

Before I'd consent to another moment

without knowing you're mine.

#595 "And Whatnot"

And I cannot fathom that you are mine. It seems illogical that after all of it – dying and whatnot – that a person like you could truly be mine. To me it's incomprehensible that I get to kiss you every day for forever. Because before you, God it wasn't even an option. I gave up on the whole damn idea. I said good riddance to love and focused on me. Not on loving me, but on maybe, occasionally liking me. And that has made all the difference. Because you and all you offer is made possible by my ability to accept what I cannot believe. Like the fact that after all of it – being born and whatnot – I am still loveable.

#436

An addict,

I found my way

back to you.

Desperate for the high

only you could give.

Forgetful of the debilitating

crash afterwards.

The self-loathing

and depression.

#437

This notebook might be as close as I ever get to you. If that's so, I'll be sure to caress every inch of you with words and allow the nuances of language to coax you to climax. Sentences will slip from my tongue to yours. And together we will make wonderful paragraphs. The you in my head becomes the poetry of my heart.

#451 "Explanations"

Hate to burst your bubble,

but I'm under no obligation

to explain myself to you.

If you don't understand me

that's your problem.

#446 "Base Instincts"

When will it end?
This inherent need to
ensure all others are
cared for.

When will it begin?
This baser urge to
care for myself.

#177

it's quite simple really.

i die a little more

every time i choose

someone's happiness

over my own

#476

She was so happy
she squirmed.
It was uncomfortable
being seen
after so long
living in the shadows.

#512

Time should mean something.
It really should. I need it to.
A choke collar. A leash.
Something, anything to hold
me back from this revelation
coming at me like a train.

Because it's not time.

Not yet.

Not for you.

#510

Life's coming together

right as I'm f

           a

              l

                l

                  i

                    n

                      g

apart.

Not the broken kind,

but the conflicted kind.

Follow my heart they say,

but what if it's no longer mine?

#527 "Rejection"

I wish I could go back. Go back to a time
when happy wasn't so damn hard. I want
to return to the moment before I stopped
believing that people really could love me.
As I was. Without additions or subtractions.
That I could hand over all the pieces – the
bad and the horrible – and they'd accept
them. No shifting through to find the
"suitable" ones.

Maybe I could. If I tried. If I really fucking
tried to hand them all over. I just…I just
don't know if I can anymore.

I'm so damn scared.

#538

It was understandable

that they didn't understand.

She didn't either.

This was just

the way she was.

#545 "Subliminal Messages"

Fine is not good. Fine is not okay.
Fine is the worst I can get. It's a
safety net for the tears. A way to
hide the torment. Fine is the shitty
Band-Aid I wear over a wound
that needs stitches.

#551 "Toxic"

She just wanted

to breathe

Her own air

Unpolluted

by expectations

#555 "The Giving Girl"

There once was a little girl

and she loved the world

and every day the world

would come and throw

rocks at her ideas, hurl

knives at her back and

play in her self-doubt...

"To Shel"

#480

I wanted to be the person who
fell into happy. The kind that
jumped in with no fear of what
was below. But I wasn't.
Somehow the lack of nerves made
me anxious. The blind leading
the blind. I knew what was
coming but couldn't see it.
How could I not when your
arms felt more like home
than any house?

#481

No goodbyes.

Not with you.

Just never ending minutes

on the clock of us.

#450

Head: "is it possible to walk a straight line and end up more lost than you were before?"

Heart: "must be, because that's what I've done."

#452

Even on the inside I was on the outside.

The quiet one that spoke when spoken to.

Some would call it a lack of trying on my

part, a blatant disregard to social norms.

But no. Once you've become one with the

universe and all its wonders it's difficult

to connect with earthly beings.

#459

Still was no longer an option. Lingering limbs languidly
watched my struggle. To be at ease, relaxed, and
refreshed was to understand the shift in paradigms.
Broken could no longer be my norm. Not when he'd
called all the piece's home. They were there waiting to
pounce predatorily on prey. Ready to rip today and
yesterday to shreds. Force me to see tomorrow. A
tomorrow where I couldn't blame the scattered shards of
my soul. Everything would be on me now. Because
you'd stupidly gone and made me whole.

#454

epic, astronomic,

otherworldly was my

failure to conform

a comet in the sky,

even the stars

couldn't touch me

#460

You forewarned me.

Many a time.

Explained repeatedly

that you were no good.

It's what made me see

me in you. I wasn't

good either. But our

bads were different.

Yours broke people.

Mine made me love

the broken.

#463

Happiness kills too.

When it's not your own.

When theirs comes at the price of yours.

When doing what you're supposed to do

feels like drowning.

A watery goodbye to all you hoped for.

All you dreamed of.

#468

Occasionally, you'll have this moment when you look in the mirror and while you don't see extraordinary, you're kinda pretty. Today you don't see the bump in your nose or how your eyes are too small. And you wish every day could be like this. That you'd wake up every morning and say to yourself, *"Can't you see you're a miracle?"*

#469

She didn't want a man she could
lose herself in. She wanted a love
that made her more herself when
she kissed him.

#479 "Burning Ring of Fire"

You walked through it

I never left

Standing still in the warmth,

allowing it to lick away

my wounds

burn away any

vestige of you

#483

Everything I wished for
and all I didn't believe
was true.

A whirlwind romance,
that was you.

#580 "To the Man Who Stole My Trust"

I don't love you anymore.

Not for a long time.

But I didn't want to hate you either.

I just want to forget you.

I want to forget that you touched me

in ways I never asked for.

I want to forget that you spoke to me

in ways no one had before.

But I could do neither of those things.

Not with all this hate.

#587 "Confinement"

I think they tried harder
with her than they ever did
with anyone else.

But no matter the material,
nothing was strong enough
to hold the ocean.

#594 "Heroes"

 she did not want to save
a world beyond saving

she wanted to save the
people who needed saving

but then again, maybe that's
the same damn thing

because a world without people
isn't much of a world at all

#456

Maybe a corpse is all I've ever been.
Noticed now only because of the putrid
scent and missing organs. Hollowed out
and decaying I can no longer pass as the
humans who've done worse to me than Time.

#462 "Chrysalis"

She admired the butterfly
and its ability to know when
comfortable creeped into
cramped

#470 "Drifting"

Sometimes it feels like I'm suffocating.
Like staying in one place is slowly killing
me. I want to run so far and so fast that
I end up somewhere no one knows my
name. A place where I can drift away
in the wind and not a soul would notice.

#474

Suffocation felt more like home
than breathing. More life sustaining
than a beating heart. And when it died
I did too.

#485 "How Do You Miss Them?"

Some people you

miss like air

others like atoms

one sustains life

the other is life

#486

I don't know about deserve or
it's about damn time. All I know
is I'm tired of one foot in, the other
dangling out. Not all ended badly
but an end is an end. Alone is alone.
I can't go back to that . . .
Not after you. You might be the
only person with whom I can have
my cake and eat it too.

#494 "J.P.K."

I've always had this disease. Never a moment passed without me feeling more than was likely warranted. It changes nothing, knowing. So after all this time . . . is it all? Probably not, but it certainly feels like all. After all this time – whatever time means, whatever all implies – I can't help but be entirely taken. With you that is. Somehow, I don't even remember falling. There was the day I didn't know your name and the day it became my favorite one to speak.

#205 "Color"

I knew you were the one when color bled into my black and white world. Never before had I noticed the way the sky bleeds and the clouds weep. Sunshine escaped my field of vision and grass was merely another place to stand. But you gave me sight when you stole my ability to breathe.

#498

After all of it
he might just be another
chapter in her incredibly long,
incredibly lonely tale.

Perhaps she wouldn't bother
turning the page.

#505 "I Love You"

Don't say it, please.

Wait too long.

Until I'm aching all

over and wanting you to

without begging you to.

Just don't say it.

Not unless you're sure.

Wait until you mean it

even if that's too long.

If it's forever . . .

#508 "How I Kiss You"

she kept her

eyes open

not because she

didn't feel it

but because she

had to see it

did he feel

it too?

#526

Even if it doesn't last

if the sky falls and the

earth opens

if every human becomes a

blip on the radar

it won't change a thing

you will forever be

my favorite drug

#529

With every day that happiness
prevailed she became more
terrified of the monsters that
lurked in the corner. They only
allowed reprieves for so long.

#533

She was homesick

not for a place

a person

but for a concept.

That somehow,

someway love

really would

prevail.

#540

There are no demons inside me.

There never were.

It was only me

and these vicious thoughts.

#544

He didn't need pens,

markers or poster boards.

He had no use for stages,

microphones or billboards.

His arms around her waist

spoke volumes as he whispered

"I love you"

#546 "Price Tag"

I let them mark me replaceable.

Now I'm the one in charge of pricing.

I wish I was worth more.

#550 "Nooks & Crannies"

God knows I'm not perfect. As far from it as I can get actually. And so, I'd never be perfect for anyone. Ever. But when night came and my head settled on your chest, when my arm wound around your waist it ceased to matter. Who gave a damn about perfect when my nooks fit in all your crannies?

#547 "Trust Issues"

My lack of distrust and suspicion

was making me terribly suspicious.

#553

I didn't want to be anything.

Anymore.

Not a thing.

Nothing.

A void.

Deep and dark.

Damp dirt.

An outside to

match my inside.

Rotting.

"I've asked you once and I'll ask again,

please give me back my coffin."

#557

There's this feeling in my chest.

Not entirely pleasant.

And I think it means I miss you.

#564

You're not alone. I want to die too.

Somedays I think a bullet to the brain

Would be less messy. Or maybe I'd go

poetic. Sliced wrists and a bathtub

full of water. How fitting would that be?

Perhaps I'll reach the end of my list

and dangle from a rope. Anything to

rid myself of this monotony.

#562

It's okay, baby.

You can bring

your demons. I'll

love them too.

#568

It's difficult not to blame myself
for the way I am. To not mark
all my oddities as faults.

Humanity hates all that's wrong
with the world: plagues, war,
famine and me.

I think then I should hate me too.
It seems only fitting if I want to
fit.

#585

Glass half full.

Glass half empty.

I'm just liquid and

air in a cup stuck

in a world that wants

to define me.

#591 "One Fish, Two Fish"

People come

and people go

some are fast

and some are slow

But they never stay.

And that is why I

believe I'm the crossroads

of people. A stop for

those finding their way

to someone who is not me.

Someone who is never me.

"A thousand thank you's Theodor"

#598 "72 Hour Hold"

I've always lived my life for others. Followed their plans and wants and needs. I do not know how to live a life for me. The real me. The one I know but don't recognize. I'm too afraid of looking in the mirror and seeing the reflection of all those thoughts I'm not supposed to have staring back at me. I'm not even sure what a life like that would look like. Or honestly how long it would last before I self-destructed. What I do know is continuing on as is isn't an option. I might self-destruct that way too.

#455

What's left of me is in pieces
scattered about, attached by
the faintest of threads. I've
lost most of me to people.

#507

I used to use places as an escape
from reality. A short break to sort
out the turmoil. Letting the beauty
around me sow life where parts of
me died. How odd it is then, that
my place is no longer a place.

It's you. . .

#457

"I love you more," she said.

Pretending like it was no big deal.
Pretending that if she said it out loud
it sounded less pathetic. Less terribly
true.

"And I always will."

#576

You are every dream I ever had

All the wishes I wasted on candles

and dandelions

You are the petals drifting in the wind

My "love me" and "love me nots"

You are the acceptance

I could never give to myself

The security without the

false sense

You are love in its purest form

And somehow you are also

mine

#537 "It's Okay"

I'm terrified of love.

I'm terrified of love.

I'm terrified –

I'm terribly in love.

#461 "Adulting"

Being an adult is just listening
to what your head says is right
over what your heart says feels
right.

#471

It happened.

There was a beat.

Small, minute, hardly decipherable.

But, yes.

Lips touched and she shook the dirt off.

Perhaps she would live after all.

Perhaps.

#509 "Fairytales"

He came to slay the dragon

But darling, that was you

#554

Don't tell me I deserve better.
Your better is different
than my better.

Instead tell me
I deserve the best.

A person who will love me
the way I want.
The way I need.

#565 "Stargazing"

It is me. No amount of running takes me
to home. Whatever that means. My soul's
too scattered. Stars thrown across the sky.
Pieces of a whole galaxy dispersed to make
something of incomprehensible beauty.
Saturn's rings and Neptune's moons. Light
years beyond human understanding. Light
years beyond human touch. I was light
years away from home. Wherever that even is.

#569 "Respiration"

I have a bad habit

of apologizing for nothing

more than the breath in

my lungs.

#574 "To Jon"

I love you.

I do.

But let me love

all of you.

Let me love the man

standing in front of

the mirror at five a.m.,

toothpaste dribbling

down his chin.

Let me love the man

broken down and tired

of a cruel, impossible

world.

Allow me to love the you

that craves escape and

adventure and roots

Show me the impossible you

the you you haven't even

shown yourself.

Let me love him,

so that I might truly

love all of you.

"That's all I ask."

#575

If all things must end

then let this be the end

to temporary

An end to uncertainty

about us

Let this end mark the

beginning of forever

#589 "The New Normal"

Perhaps crazy is all she ever wanted to be.
Crazy enough to live. Crazy enough to love.
Crazy enough to fall and get back up, fail
and keep trying. She wanted to be crazy
enough to chase her dreams no matter the
opposition she faced. She wanted to be
manically insane in a society that took
such pleasure in normality.

#473

I can't fit with anyone

until I learn to fit

inside myself.

Something I fear

will never happen.

There's too much of me

to cram in an

insignificant body.

#488 "Green Thumb"

I was always fooling myself
believing that if I used enough water
flowers would surely grow

how stupid could I be?
you were just another in
my garden of weeds

#506

Without you
I lost touch
rustling through pages
frantically trying to
remember my

                  place
Life became moments
with

         and

without you.

A bookmark of sorts,
you kept me grounded
in this moment. When
and when you weren't
present…

#531 "Introductions"

That pause. That breathe of air before a known stranger becomes an acquaintance. She fills it. Every time. Fearful of what he might or might not say if given the reins.

#543

I fear being defined
by my fear

That somehow I'll let it
tether me to the now

To this moment I'm
awfully familiar with

#556

When I look at you, it stops.
Every chaotic thought, every
pointless doubt, every negative
feeling. They die. You are the
death of me.

You are living.

#567

I was going with the flow. My flow. Being flexible doesn't always mean following the crowd. Sometimes it simply means becoming your own stream. A quiet, steady stream. A profoundly capable stream. And when the time is right, you can join the river once more.

#579

You thought I'd be grateful?
Grateful that you had the audacity
to rip off what I painstakingly
sewed to my face. No one gave you
the right. I didn't know what was
behind this flesh that wasn't really
flesh. So neither would you.

Just stop trying.

#592 "Me I Am"

I will always be missing you.
In some fashion or another.

When there's space between
us I will miss the me I am
when I hold your hand.

When I hold your hand I will
miss the me I am when there
is space between us.

I will always be missing me.
In some fashion or another.

I will always be hoping the
me I am is just one me.

#599 "Advice From An Introvert"

You need to be reminded that you are indeed alive. You need the out of breath, the dry tears, the skinned knees. You need the laughter that breaks your ribs. You need the good cries and the painful cries and all the cries in between. You need a wall hopped, a skinned knee, a smile on your face because you made it to the other side. You need all these annoyingly human things, because otherwise you forget that your heart is beating and your lungs are breathing. You. Are. Alive. As frustrating as this is at times, you just are. So let go and live a little.

#334 "Promises From An Introvert"

If nothing else, I give you understanding. There's no hole too deep, no hallway too dark to send me packing. Glass is sharp but I'm not afraid to bleed for those I love. My monsters will scare off yours and maybe yours will scare mine too. And then it'll be just the two of us sitting in mutual understanding. If not peace.

#472 "Inquiries of the Important Kind"

Why does doing what's best for me

have such negative associations?

Does it imply that I'm selfish?

Choosing my own happiness over others?

Or is this kind of self-love allowed?

#492 "Cellblock"

His arms were not

the prison so many

others were.

And that was everything…

#530

I'm not the jealous type.

Just the

"I can't possibly be enough"

type

#548 "For Frost"

I'm on this road less traveled

A little less lonely than before

A tad bit more afraid

that maybe I wasn't

not this whole time

and I'm finally deciding

to take the road less traveled.

#552 "Ignorance Isn't Bliss"

That's enough. Close the door.

I don't want to want anymore.

Give me ignorance. It ain't bliss

but it's better. You were supposed

to give me better. You were supposed

to give me bliss.

That's enough. I should've known

not to open that door. I didn't want

to want anymore.

#558

Light it up.

Light it all up.

Gasoline and matches.

Do it right.

Burn it to the ground.

Maybe then I'll finally

be able to see.

#571

It's happening again
The beginning of the end
No longer unique, but odd
All the quirks that marked me
intriguing now label me difficult

There's no place for me.
Not in your life, with your people.
I just don't fit.

It's okay. I'm not mad.
You can do it. Back to the shelf.
A display item.
Do not touch.

#584

She wanted to make her mark
on a place that would swallow her
whole. Bones and all. Wasn't that
beautiful? Wasn't it gloriously
selfless? Living for a place that
would forget you the moment lungs
stopped working. That's love.
The real, unbridled kind.

#493

As if by some magic,

without her ever having

to utter a word, he knew

just what to do to

make her speak

And just where to touch

to make her sigh

#340 "A Request"

Just for tonight I want to forget what it is to be my own person. Steal the s p a c e between my fingers and the breath from my lungs. Capture my beating heart and pin my shaking arms. Then settle. Settle so closely that even we don't know what we were before. Alter me with a touch. Consume me with a sigh. Engrave this moment – where you weren't you and I wasn't me – on the fabric of time.

#534 "Dropping Knowledge"

A cage made of love

is still a cage

#535

You weren't a life vest.
You didn't save me from
the chaos inside.
You did something better.
Something I can never
properly thank you for.
You allowed me to
coexist with my demons.
You were my oxygen tank.

#549

And then the day came

when I realized it was me

and alone was what

I was meant to be

#570 "Inquiries of the Important Kind 2"

Maybe I was running. But what did it matter?
If escape was what I needed they should just let
me have it. Would it hurt them for me to be
happy? Would it really be that bad?

#573

I go days. Weeks. Months even
without writing a single line.

Then it happens: emotions.
And all I can do is try and
keep up with the torrent of words.

#583

I am not easy to love.

Do not mistake me

I'm not difficult either.

I'm somewhere in between

annoyingly understanding

and painfully stubborn.

I will accept all there is to you.

Unconditionally. I will love

your flaws and make no move

to morph you into my idea of

perfection. There will be no need.

Because I will coax you to growth.

Love has a way of taking a seed

and turning it into something

magnificent.

#600

What scares you about loving scares me too. You hand
over all these broken bits, the puzzle pieces without
partners, the peas with no pods and you just have to trust
them. You have to trust that they'll love all the odds and
ends. That they won't discard fragments of you. That if
anything, they'll add to you. They'll mend the broken,
be partners to the puzzle and find the pod.

#601

I don't want to be bothered by the things I cannot change. But it drives me mad knowing there's nothing special about me. What I've traced was just a path forged by other's fingertips. Where I sleep is already broken in (I suppose I should thank them for that). But I really don't want to. I don't want them. I don't want to know they wanted you. Had you. Because you wanted them too. I want us. Just us. And a newness that sends life pulsating through this corpse I call home. But some part or another will always be rotting because, like everyone else, there's nothing special about me. I'm just a vessel looking for another vessel to bring me back to life.

#602 "The Messy Truth"

I know they say time heals and distance makes the heart grow fonder but we have nothing to heal and no reason for distance. And...and I'm so damn scared. Scared that time will "heal" something not broken and steal your ability to miss me. I'm terrified that distance will make you feel anything but fonder.

#603 "PDA"

His words, his actions. They would never be enough.
Not really. It didn't matter if he showed it. She would
always need a little bit more. Something more tangible.
Something touchable. She needed to lose herself under
the sheets and see that he was lost too. Words and
actions were nothing without the touches that told her
this was real.

-private displays of affection

#604

I'd like to be caught up in the moments that make me feel. Anything. Anything but this lackluster void I've made my home. I want to burn down in an all-consuming rage. Drown in a never-ending ocean of grief. I want to soar through the clouds on wings of happiness and hit rock bottom when melancholy enters my world. I want to feel anything and everything that reminds me why living is better than this slow death I've condemned myself to.

#605

Faded, chipped, rusted.

Call it what you will.

It's all the same.

Same remedy. Scratch that.

Same damn bit of denial.

A new coat of paint.

Problem solved.

No true colors to be seen...

#607

I've got this irrational fear that if I'm not present I won't exist. That if I can't be seen I won't be heard. That if physical is taken out of the equation so is emotional.

I've got this somewhat rational fear that you can't possibly miss me as much as I miss you.

#608

I swear I tried. I did. I really fucking did, but my souls too odd a shape to mesh with other people's. It's a little too rough around the edges. A tad bit too abrasive. Too damn enlightened for them to handle.

I tried. I did. I really fucking did. But they didn't.

#609

I want you to be happy.

But I want you to be

happy with me.

I don't know if that makes

me selfless, selfish or

just human.

#610

What really has me trembling, shaking in my boots, absolutely incapacitated is that there will never be another you. I've got today. As many todays as you'll allow me to make this right. To keep it as right for you as it feels for me. Because god it does. Nothing has ever felt righter than this all-encompassing terror coursing through my veins. Nothing will ever feel righter than the moments I spend loving you.

#611

Without him ever having
to be present she realized
he was the one. She was
alone but not lonely.

Not anymore.

#613 "Happily Ever After"

And they lived happily ever after…
Or so they say. But they don't show
do they? They neglect to mention the
excruciating experience of merging
your life, your heart, your soul
with another.

Happily ever after. After the pain.
After the heartbreak. After discovering
that you might be too damn different.

#614

You cannot measure the missing,
but if you could I think mine
would be bigger. More depth,
height, width, length. More of
everything. It is bigger than me.
My missing. It's bigger than the
days and weeks and months.
And yours is bearable. And that is
sad.

#616 "DOA"

"The only life in this room
is of the electric kind."

And that sentence never used

to bother me so damn much.

Where are the beating hearts?

Yours and mine.

A sleepover with no attendees.

Not even me.

A body in a bed.

A blanket for a bag.

Breathless.

#617

I know nothing of reality.
Whether or not mine is
the same as yours or
anything close to alike.
I don't know much about
existence or the meaning
of life. All I know is I want
to know nothing with you.

"A TLC Production"

#619

She's the monster under the bed

The boogey man in the closet

She's the alleyway shadow dogging

their every step

She's all society deemed scary

because they simply couldn't

understand different

#620 "Daily Mantra"

I'm the problem and that's okay.

I'm the problem and that's okay.

I'm the prob—

I'm different and that doesn't

equal problem. Who I am is

okay.

Now repeat.

#621

I want to get out of this funk that's not a funk. Because, really this is just me. I'd like to write anything other than this melancholic bullshit spilling out of me like blood. All I've got it *like to's* and *want to's* waiting around to be fulfilled but I'm too busy cutting my wrists to notice.

"this is how I kill myself when I want to die"

#623

Pop the cork. Break open the dam.

"Let it out," they say. And you do.

Bubbly's everywhere. The village is flooded.

The room's a mess. Hundred's dead.

And you're among them. Drowned

in the emotions you tried to swallow.

#624 "A Case of the Feels"

And in an instant she knew why
it was called "catching feels".
Far from self-preserving, it attacked
sanity and conscious thought. These
feelings invaded all there was to her
until only he remained. It was maddening.
Not a day or night could go by without
her wondering what he was wondering
and hoping it was about her.

#625

They don't ever stop, do they? The growing pains.
It only becomes more unbearable in this fully grown
body with no give. You grow, you change, you morph
and this useless vessel stays the same. What should
be home becomes a prison holding in all that screams
for a way out.

#626

I am everything that's happened to me.

I am all the ways I let their actions ruin me. I am the nights I spent balling my eyes out instead of sleeping. I am all the screams my pillow kept for me. I am the thoughts one should never have to think. I am the coward who couldn't follow through. But I am also all the ways *I survived* the adversity. I am the compassion I showed others. I am the words I wrote and the darkness I shared. I am open ears and a willing shoulder. I am human. Ruined and built back up differently. Perhaps less effectively. Perhaps more.

#627

Nothing will ever confuse me more than the fact that sometimes what loves you breaks you. And even though they couldn't touch you with gentle hands they really didn't mean to harm. It will never make sense to me that some people destroy everything about the person they love and wonder why they can't recognize them anymore. I don't think I'll ever be able to grasp that they really did love them though. They did.

#628

Your name sounds

the same as home

to my ears

#629

So this is what missing is. This inescapable,

indescribable feeling that something is just

a little off. That there's a piece of you gone.

Something rather important to your makeup.

Missing is this blank hole with a name. I've

got to fill it and only you will do.

#631 "She"

Street art was his

hearts delight

museum worthy

but not fond

of frames

#632

I am sorry though. I'm sorry that some days I look at you and cannot smile. I'm sorry that occasionally all I see is everything I'm giving up. Not the me before the you but the me after, because there's no way this can last. And of everything that's what I'm most sorry for. Because you're so sure it will. You're delusional and in love with me and you think that'll be enough. But I'm prone to sacrifice and I'll throw myself on this pen again and again to end the torture.

#634 "Hello Again"

I think that I am pretty today.

There's something about these eyes.

Bloodshot and glistening. Sad doe eyes

that feel like home. I missed this girl.

This beautifully melancholy girl.

Thank you for giving her back to me.

#635 "On Losing My Bestfriend"

The saddest thing any of us will ever have to go through is the realization that we don't exist. Not to them anyhow. It's the moment we realize we've died. At least the us that was a part of them. And that's not something you can come back from. You can't return the same from the grave. There'll be organs missing and flesh more at home in the earth than on muscle. The saddest thing any of us will ever have to do is go on living after death. Because we are still apart of other half rotting humans that need us to keep them resembling something bipedal.

#636 "Humpty Dumpty"

I'm falling to pieces

and there's not enough

glue in the world

to put me back

together again

#637

I hate you. Just a little. It's really little, the hate, but it's there. I hate you because you gave me clear blue skies and safe nights. I hate you because you gave me a heartbeat to fall asleep to and fingertips to wake to. I hate that you made yourself my home, my rock and my anchor. I hate so much that all the things you gave me marked you reliable and still I was wrong. Because I expected things from you you couldn't give and I hate you because I was disappointed when I knew better. I hate you because I love you. I hate you because I will always forgive you for the ways you cannot be for me. I hate you because you gave me happy and I'm so much emptier now that I knew it.

#638

Swimming would always
be more exhausting
than drowning for her

She saw more beauty
in surrendering to the water
than she ever would in
fighting the waves.

#639

It's okay to admit it. Their words aren't doing their intended job. "You're not different, you're ---" Unique. Special. One of a kind. Fill in the blank. But we're all one of a kind. You and I are just the one of a kinds that don't mesh with the other one of a kinds. "You're a solo act. You stand ---" Alone, I know. No need to remind me. All these synonyms, all these phrases to erase the word they hate just a bit. Because it's detonation doesn't matter. Not when the connotation is so devastating. You are different. And while that's the most incredible thing anyone could ever be afflicted with, you won't know this for a while. Maybe forever. So here I am, telling you screw their fillers. Their synonyms and phrases. You are unique, special, one of a kind AND different and those are all wonderful ways to be described.

#640

That's how love works though doesn't it?

There's no timing to it. No waiting for the

right moment, for solid ground and a

balanced life. *BANG.* It just happens.

One moment you're living life and the next

you're doing the life thing with the love

of your life.

#593

I'm just using words

to paint pretty pictures

with the pain life handed me.

Something good had to

come out of this mess.

Namesake:

A Fellow Outcast. I'd like to think that when the name came to me it was some epiphany. Some incredibly profound moment. But I'd be lying to myself. It came to me the way quiet revelations do. It was a whisper over my skin, an understanding in my pen. I'd reached the end of my first poetry book, *Angels & Inner Demons*, and an Author's Note just felt right. But how to sign off? N. Avila seemed too informal. Nikki Avila felt too unoriginal.

In essence I was more than myself. Some of these poems were from a different life, a different me and so the note shouldn't be written from I. I thought it should be from someone that was everyone. An outcast. A Fellow Outcast. Because who among us has never felt like a pariah? Who had never felt the strains of a box in which they could not fit? If I could reach the outcast in everyone and remind them that they were not alone than my task would be filled. It became so simple when I thought of it that way.

I was moments away from signing The Outcast, but that wouldn't be true. We are, each and every one of us, an outcast in one way or another. Who was I to own the name Outcast? But A Fellow Outcast? Well that was alright. That was inclusive. That was something I could live with.

-A Fellow Outcast

For more exclusive content go to

afellowoutcast.blogspot.com

Follow the author on Instagram

@nikki.avila

and on Twitter

@nikki_avila96

www.ingramcontent.com/pod-product-compliance
Lightning Source LLC
Chambersburg PA
CBHW060239050426
42448CB00009B/1507